Maurice S. Baldwin

Life in a Look

Maurice S. Baldwin

Life in a Look

ISBN/EAN: 9783337053925

Printed in Europe, USA, Canada, Australia, Japan

Cover: Foto ©ninafisch / pixelio.de

More available books at **www.hansebooks.com**

MAURICE S. BALDWIN,

Rector of the Parish of Montreal: Canon of the Cathedral.

MONTREAL:
DAWSON BROTHERS, PUBLISHERS.

1879.

PRINTED BY
J. THEO. ROBINSON, successor to J. STARKE & CO.

LIFE IN A LOOK.

Chapter I:
THE NECESSITY OF THE NEW BIRTH.

Chapter II:
THE NATURE OF THE NEW BIRTH.

Chapter III:
REGENERATION IN ITS CONNECTION WITH CHRIST ON THE CROSS.

Conclusion:
"LOOKING UNTO JESUS;" OR, GROWTH IN GRACE.

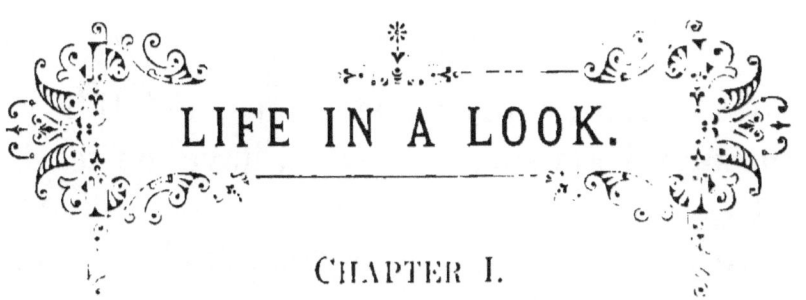

LIFE IN A LOOK.

CHAPTER I.

THE NECESSITY OF THE NEW BIRTH.

DEAR Reader, am I wrong in supposing you wish to know HOW TO BE SAVED?

If I am, and you really care nothing for the subject, please, nevertheless, read on. In these pages you will find nothing but that which really concerns YOURSELF; and that which concerns ourselves demands at least our careful attention. If, on the contrary, you really wish for this knowledge, then the very *first* truth you have to learn is: THE VITAL NECESSITY OF THE NEW BIRTH. This was the first doctrine our blessed Lord taught Nicodemus, and this is the first, I am sure, He would have me teach YOU.

In the third chapter of St. John's Gospel we read that Nicodemus, a learned ruler of the Jews, came to Jesus by night apparently to enquire of Him the way of salvation. "*Rabbi,*" said Nicodemus, "*we know that Thou art a teacher come from God: for no man can do these miracles that Thou doest, except God be with him.*" There is much to admire in Nicodemus. He evidently had far juster views of the Lord Jesus than many of his own nation. The Pharisees used to say of Christ: "*He casteth out devils by Beelzebub the chief of the devils.*" Others were heard to say: "*He deceiveth the people.*" But Nicodemus uttered no such blasphemy; on the contrary, he thought the blessed Saviour was a true Prophet. He comes to Him and says: Rabbi, we know that Thou art a TEACHER COME FROM GOD. It was a great truth to know, even though he knew no more than this, for certainly Christ was a teacher, and much more than a teacher; He was what no prophet ever was,—not even such men as

Isaiah or Daniel—THE LIGHT OF THE WORLD. Thousands in our day go as far as this, and here halt. Jews who reject Christ as their Redeemer, but yet in some sense consider Him a great Reformer; sceptics who would subvert, if possible, half the Bible; professing Christians, ignorant of the *life* that is in Christ—all may be heard to-day addressing the Lord Jesus in the exact words of Nicodemus: Rabbi, we know Thou art *a teacher* come from God. Nothing more; not exclusively THE teacher, but simply one of the many teachers come from God to enlighten and to bless the world. What Nicodemus had to learn—what thousands of professing Christians need to know; what indeed the whole world shall yet be made to see—is, that Christ is *more* than a teacher come from God; He is THE RESURRECTION AND THE LIFE. Eternal Life dwells IN HIM, "for as the Father hath life in Himself, so hath He given to the Son to have Life in himself." Therefore, until we know Christ as our LIFE, we know Him not. "He that hath the Son hath LIFE, and he that hath not the Son of God hath NOT life." To this bear all the prophets witness; to this our Lord Himself and His Apostles unite their testimony " *That God hath given to us eternal life, and this life is in His Son.*"

And now, I will ask you carefully to weigh our Lord's answer to Nicodemus. It was one in every way momentous, and as such should seriously be considered. Its striking peculiarity is, that it seems to have no apparent connection with the words of Nicodemus; and yet, doubtless, it was the exact answer he needed—the one best suited to his spiritual wants. "*I am He*," saith Christ, "*that searcheth the hearts;*" and assuredly in this instance he did so, for, looking deep down into the heart of Nicodemus, He instantly saw what the wants of his soul were, and these He immediately meets. The learned Jew had begun the interview by saying: " Rabbi, we know that Thou art a teacher come from God." This remark the Saviour passes by, and, addressing Himself to the great truth of which Nicodemus was most profoundly ignorant, namely, his need of a new birth, He utters these memorable words: " VERILY, VERILY I SAY UNTO THEE, EXCEPT

A MAN BE BORN AGAIN, HE CANNOT SEE THE KINGDOM OF GOD."

These words of the Lord Jesus are as directly addressed to *you*, dear reader, as they were to Nicodemus, that is, if you have not yet experienced this new birth of which Christ speaks. Therefore, seeing they are for *your* everlasting life, and that the speaker is none other than Jesus Christ Himself, I implore you both earnestly and prayerfully to weigh them.

Observe, first Christ goes to the very root of things. He says spiritual LIFE begins with spiritual BIRTH.

Men see physical activity all about them, and they know that in each case this activity had its origin in the *birth* of those who are now so incessantly engaged. There was first birth, then development, then manhood, and with manhood ceaseless industry of mind and body. In spiritual matters, however, thousands who admit to the full all the above, will persist in reversing this well known law: for the idea to which they most tenaciously cling is, that if they can only DO those things which are pleasing in God's sight, that *then*

God will grant them life. In spiritual matters, as in physical, life is *first*, activity afterwards.

You meet a man anxiously pressing toward the cemetery, and, stopping him, ask the cause. "I have just obtained," he says, "a large contract, and want men to enable me to fulfil it." "But why go, of all places, to the cemetery?" you again ask—"none there but the dead." "The very reason why I *do* go," he replies—"unemployed hands there, sir! unemployed hands! I have something for them to do." "The man's mad," you say, and turn away, feeling melancholy at the shipwreck of his intellect. No doubt he is, but not more so, in a spiritual sense, than he who addresses a whole congregation dead in trespasses and sins, as if they were all LIVING members of Jesus Christ, and, taking all the precepts of the Christian life, asks those who have not yet begun to BREATHE, to carry them out in their daily lives. How often, for instance, do we hear this text given out:—"*So run that ye may obtain*," and then the glorious and completed salvation of the Son of God is described as a race in which the swiftest runner alone obtains eternal life. The congregations, largely composed of people absolutely dead before God, are then exhorted by all means to run this race, and by all means to obtain this life. It is just this outrageous perversion of the Word of God which utterly misleads thousands; it bolsters them up with the false idea that they are the children of God, when they are not; it is a going to the DEAD to give them employment; an assigning labor to those whom the Resurrection and the Life has not yet raised into being, and the result is utter and hopeless failure. Spiritual life only begins with spiritual birth, and as those to whom I allude have not been *born* of the Spirit, they can no more fulfil the precepts of the Christian life than you, dear reader, can fly with the eagle, or race with the lightning of heaven.

'Secondly:' These words of Christ clearly prove the UTTER HELPLESSNESS OF ALL HUMAN EFFORT, and the ABSOLUTE SOVEREIGNTY OF GOD.

One thing may safely be said of Nicodemus, and that is, he was thoroughly in earnest. There was therefore nothing within the range of human possibility he would not gladly have done at the suggestion of our Lord. Had Christ told him his sorrow for his past sins was not deep enough, he would have humbled himself in the profoundest abjections; had Christ commanded his immediate surrender of all his goods to feed the poor, doubtless he would have hasted to obey; but our Lord says none of these things. He gives him, in fact, NOTHING TO DO; nothing to please his vanity, or stimulate his self-conceit. He prescribes no fasts, no tears, no human effort; only utters these words—so dark and inexplicable to the mind of Nicodemus—"*Except a man be born again he cannot see the kingdom of God.*" Now, as long as a man thinks there *is* some*thing* by the doing of which he can procure his salvation—no matter what that something may be—he will never despair. If he fail in his effort to-day, he will only try the more to-morrow; but when at last the conviction is forced upon him that he is absolutely DEPENDENT on the Holy Spirit, and that he must be BORN AGAIN, he sees, for the first time, that God requires something utterly **BEYOND** his power. Now a man may make the most costly sacrifices, he may even go as far as laying down his life in the fond hope of pleasing God thereby, but there is *one* thing he can *not* do, and that is, effect his own new birth. Yet our Lord says positively, "Except a man be born again, he CANNOT SEE the kingdom of God." It follows, therefore, that the unsaved sinner is thrown back on the absolute sovereignty of God. Effort *in any direction* on his part is utterly impossible. This only can he do:—as speechless, lay his hand upon his mouth; as humbled, bend down his face to the dust; and thus, in silence, *listen*, while GOD SPEAKS.

But many people object to this, and say: Does not St. Paul command, "Work out your own salvation with fear and trembling"? and does not this precept of his teach us that salvation is the result of a life-long struggle? By no means. To whom did the Apostle utter this command? Was it to the Court of Nero?—to the gladiators of the circus?—to men dead in trespasses and sins?

No, it was to the Philippian Christians—to men and women rejoicing in the truth. His very letter is thus addressed: "To all the SAINTS in Christ Jesus which are at Philippi." Now, no man can be a saint while the wrath of God abides on him, and the wrath of God abides on *all* who are not "*justified by faith:*" it abides, in other words, on all who are unsaved; but the Philippians were saints, they were therefore "*justified by faith,*" and as such were saved—were BORN AGAIN. What then does the Apostle mean when he says, "*Work out your own salvation with fear and trembling?*" In explanation of this, two facts have to be borne in mind, first,—While all the justified will be *saved*, they will not all receive a *crown;* many of them will be saved "*so as by fire;*" and, secondly,—Salvation from wrath is only part of our redemption. Redemption really implies life in union with our Lord Jesus Christ, liberation from the servitude of sin, and victory over Satan and the world. By the expression, "Work out your own salvation," the Apostle means the salvation you have already received—not the salvation you are to obtain—and we are to do so " with fear and trembling," lest we should dishonor our Lord, and LOSE the recompense of the reward.

This idea is well expressed by the Church of England in her Xth Article : " Wherefore we have no power to do good works, pleasant and acceptable to God, without the grace of God by Christ preventing (going before) us, that we may have a good will, and working with us, when we have that good will."

No, dear reader, there is nothing you can DO, but as LOST and HELPLESS, listen to the words of Christ.

Thirdly : *Our Lord's words teach the ritual* NECESSITY *of the new birth.*

Whatever opinions we may hold about the new birth, there is *one* point on which all must be agreed, and that is, ITS VITAL NECESSITY. Our Lord does not say: Except a man be born again, it will be ages of time before he enters the kingdom of God ; nor, Except a man be born again, he will never enjoy the *same* degree of glory as one who has; nor, Except a man be born again he shall not *enter* the kingdom of God; but, "Except a man be born again, he cannot SEE," that is, comprehend, "the kingdom of God."

You will therefore see the absolute necessity of *your* obtaining this new birth. Whatever its meaning—whatever event it points to—its vital importance is awfully evident. Our Lord says: "Without it no man can even SEE the kingdom of God."

Fourthly: *Our Lord's words teach us that the birth He refers to is a* HEAVENLY *birth.*

Literally, the word "*again*" is FROM ABOVE. Now, we have all had one birth *from beneath*, that is, our natural physical birth, when we came into the world; but Christ says this first physical birth is not enough; we need another—one from above. When therefore we have this birth from above, we are, in our Lord's language, born of the Spirit; we have experienced this wondrous birth without which no man can see the kingdom of God. I would have you also notice that the two births, the physical and the spiritual, never occur TOGETHER. Man was altogether "born in sins," with a "heart deceitful above all things, and desperately wicked." Indeed so strongly is this insisted on by the inspired writers, that St. Paul tells us, in the 8th chapter of Romans: " *The mind of the flesh* (the carnal mind in our version) is ENMITY AGAINST GOD." It is not merely *at* enmity, but the very *principle*—enmity itself. St. Paul further affirms two other truths of this natural heart of ours: *first*, " that it is not subject to the law of God," and *second*, " neither indeed CAN be." It is not subject to the law of God either in the regenerate or unregenerate, and this impossibility to be subject to God's law comes from the very nature of its own being—a nature which is always in a state of irreconcilable hostility to God.

Born therefore with such a heart as this, you need, dear reader, to be BORN AGAIN; and it must be apparent to you that no one receives the two births, that is, the physical and the spiritual, at one and the same time; for then our spiritual birth could no more be a matter of injunction or command than our physical; we would all be *regenerated* people from our very entrance into the world, and no one would need to be saved, for all would be saved already.

In connection with this subject, I wish to draw your attention to an expression, very common among people, but, at the same time, one thoroughly unscriptural. I refer to the oft-used phrase. "a *change* of heart." Now such an expression as this does not occur in the whole range of Scripture. We find in Daniel that a watcher said, concerning Nebuchadnezzar: "*Let his heart be changed from man's, and let a beast's heart be given unto him;*" but from Genesis to Revelation there is no passage which teaches that God CHANGES the natural evil heart into a GOOD HEART. We find such expressions as a "new heart," "another heart," a "new spirit," but never a *changed heart*. The truth is, God never mends, renews, or changes the natural heart. What He says, is—"A NEW heart also will I give you, and a NEW spirit will I put within you." Our Lord, therefore, in speaking to Nicodemus, did not say: Except a man's heart be renewed or changed, he shall not see the kingdom of God, but,—"Except a man be BORN AGAIN."

Chapter II.

THE NATURE OF THE NEW BIRTH.

THE Saviour's words fell on heavy ears. Not the faintest idea of the truth He uttered passed through the mind of Nicodemus; for, supposing our Lord to be speaking of a physical birth, he asks with astonishment: "How can a man be born when he is old? can he enter the second time into his mother's womb and be born?" To this the Redeemer makes the memorable reply: "Verily, verily, I say unto thee, except a man be born of WATER and of THE SPIRIT, he cannot enter into the kingdom of God." Our first enquiry therefore must be:—What did our Lord mean by the expression

BORN OF WATER?

Water occurs in Scripture as signifying the perfect washing which Christ effects in the soul, including not only His purgation of our sins by His most precious blood, but also his cleansing us from our own natural selves, that is, our carnal and deceitful hearts. The signification of the word "water" is not uniform throughout Scripture; for instance, in Jer. i. 13, water is spoken of as a figure of *God Himself:* "They have forsaken Me, the fountain of living waters." As descriptive of *military power:* "Behold waters rise up out of the north, and shall be an overflowing flood." (Jer. xlvii. 2.) As emblematic of deep and terrible *affliction:* "Deep calleth unto deep at the noise of Thy waterspouts: all Thy waves and Thy billows are gone over me." (Psalm xlii. 7.) Especially of the awful sorrows of Christ: "Save Me, O God; for the waters are come in unto My soul. I am come into deep waters, where the floods overflow Me. Let Me be delivered from them that hate Me, and out of the deep waters. Let not the waterflood overflow Me, neither let the deep swallow Me up." (Psalm lxix. 1, 2, 14, 15.) Of God's judgment on the sinner, thus Eliphaz says to Job: "Thou hast sent widows away empty. * * * Therefore snares are round about thee, * * * and abundance of waters cover thee." (Job xxii. 9, 10, 11.) Of the Holy Spirit, thus our Lord says: "He that believeth on Me, as the Scripture hath said, out of his belly shall flow rivers of living water. But this spake He of the Spirit, which they that believe on Him should receive." (John vii. 38, 39.) It is mentioned as that which typically cleanses. Thus God says by the mouth of His servant Ezekiel: "Then will I sprinkle clean water upon you, and ye shall be clean: from all your filthiness, and from all your idols will I cleanse you." (Ezekiel xxxvi. 25.) And in this sense was it so used in the brazen Laver, and "water of separation,"—two objects in the Levitical economy of the deepest spiritual import. Leaving, however, the types and shadows of the Law, we find the word "water" repeatedly occurring in other parts of Scripture, as a striking and beautiful type of the Gospel of Jesus Christ. For instance, in these words spoken by Isaiah: "Ho, every one that thirsteth, come ye to the waters, and he that hath no money; come ye, buy and eat; yea, come, buy wine and milk without money and without price," we have an invitation for all who are in want to come and partake of the rich bounty of the Gospel feast. The "waters" here mentioned are the blessings of the covenant of grace—the unsearchable riches of Christ, made known to us in that Gospel which is the power of God unto salvation to every one that believeth. When our Lord was upon earth, men had ocular demonstration of His power; they saw for themselves His astounding miracles; they had the evidence of his actual being before their eyes; and therefore in many cases their faith was the result of sight. Now, all this is changed, and men are asked to believe, not on the evidence of that which they see, but on the credibility of that which they hear. Even when our Lord was on earth, He asserted the superior blessedness of that faith which arose from hearing, without actual sight: "Thomas," said He, "because thou hast seen Me, thou hast believed: blessed are they that have not seen, yet have believed." Christ is now on high, seated in glory at the right hand of the Father, but before He ascended to so exalted a place, He assured

His disciples that it was expedient for them that He should go away and leave them, and the reason He assigns for so great a change is, that the Dispensation which was immediately to follow was to be the Dispensation of the Spirit. He was no longer visibly to tread the earth; men were no longer with their own eyes to see Him raising the dead, healing the sick, calming the sea, feeding the hungry, or casting out unclean spirits with His word. In His room was to be the Holy Spirit, not working on the external organs, but convincing the understanding and winning the heart. And this the Spirit does, not to draw sinners to *Himself*, but to the *Lord Jesus Christ;* for, speaking of the Spirit, our Lord says: " The Spirit of Truth, which proceedeth from the Father, He shall TESTIFY OF ME." (John xv. 26.) The work therefore of the Comforter on earth is to uplift alike in the heart of the saved and unsaved, the person, the work, and the kingdom of the Lord Jesus Christ. He labors, therefore, to bring home to the soul of the sinner God's record concerning His Son; to convince him of his unutterable need of that salvation which the Father has provided in Christ; to accept the eternal gift; to believe and live forever. But how can the Spirit testify without a testimony? How can He speak to the heart of the sinner unless He have a message from the Father to convey to it? A testimony, a message, he must have; and that testimony and that message He has in the BIBLE, the *word* of the eternal God. The Holy Spirit therefore in leading a lost one to Christ, does not bring before his eyes physical miracles; nor does He scare him with dreams, or overcome his judgment with appeals to the sensuous and emotional. On the contrary, He speaks to the conscience simply and alone through the testimony of God's word. And man knows not how, but suddenly, and with great power, a passage of Scripture is brought home to him. It is no new revelation, but a well known verse he has read and heard a thousand times before, but it now comes down into his soul with a reality and conviction unfelt in the past. He wonders what it all means; it is the Holy Ghost applying God's written word to his conscience; opening his eyes and arousing his mind to hear the eternal truths which make for everlasting life.

Such then is the way in which the Spirit acts; His message is the word of God, and His work is to apply this word to the consciences of those who either read it themselves or have it preached to them by others.

Thus we see clearly the way in which people are saved. There is first the Bible, the word of God, declaring the way in which alone God will justify sinners, namely, through faith in the Lord Jesus Christ; and secondly, there is the Holy Spirit to apply that word with saving efficacy to the heart of man. The WORD and the HOLY SPIRIT are therefore God's two great agents in the salvation of men. If the Holy Spirit were alone on earth without the word of God, He could not bear testimony to the truth concerning Jesus Christ; and if, on the other hand, the Bible were by itself on earth without the presence of the Spirit, no one would be saved, " for the natural man (that is, the unrenewed heart) receiveth not the things of the Spirit of God: for they are FOOLISHNESS unto him; and he CANNOT know them, because they are spiritually discerned." (1 Cor. ii. 14). Such being the case, we might expect that our Lord would declare this truth in such a discourse as we have before us, and this assuredly He has done in these words: "Except a man be born of water and of the Spirit, he cannot enter into the kingdom of God."

I have already shown how many in Scripture are the significations of the word "water," but I now wish to add that often, when the Holy Ghost wishes to describe the refreshing and invigorating nature of the Gospel, He does so by picturing it under the form of that well known element. For instance, in Isaiah lv. 1, God says: "Ho, every one that thirsteth, come ye to the WATERS." Now here the prophet is announcing the glorious Gospel, afterwards to be revealed in the coming of the Lord Jesus. He describes under the word "waters" the unspeakable blessings of the "everlasting covenant" mentioned in the third verse, and this everlasting covenant is, and can be nothing else, than the Testament or Gospel of the grace of God. The vision of the "holy waters," issuing from under the threshold of the Temple, was a striking and beautiful simile by which God, through Ezekiel, foretold the publication of the Gospel of peace. (Ezek. xlvii. 1.) So too the "living waters" of Zech. xiv. 8, point to the great truth that during the period of millennial blessedness, Jerusalem is to be the spiritual centre of the earth, and that from it are to go forth "living waters" for the salvation of the Gentile world. In like manner, the very last invitation we have in the Bible, speaks of the glorious Gospel under the word "water:" "Whosoever will, let him take the WATER OF LIFE freely." (Rev. xxii. 17.) Thus we see that one of the many uses of this word is to bring before us the blessed and life-giving qualities of the Gospel of Jesus Christ.

That this is the correct interpretation, is confirmed to us by the fact that the inspired writers ascribe *regeneration* to the power of the Gospel. St. Paul, writing to the Corinthians, says: "In Christ Jesus I have BEGOTTEN YOU THROUGH THE GOSPEL." (1 Cor. iv. 15.) So also St. James: "Of His own will BEGAT HE US WITH THE WORD

OF TRUTH." (James i. 18.) St. Peter's testimony is also to the same effect: "Being BORN AGAIN, not of corruptible seed, but of incorruptible, by THE WORD OF GOD which liveth and abideth for ever." (1 Peter i. 23.) Previously, in this chapter, the same Apostle states: "Blessed be the God and Father of our Lord Jesus Christ, which according to His abundant mercy hath BEGOTTEN US AGAIN unto a lively hope by the resurrection of Jesus Christ from the dead." We are said to have been begotten again unto a lively hope by the resurrection, from the fact of its being the grand confirmation of the Gospel; the sublime miracle by which the Gospel was proved to be of God, and by which our faith in it is triumphantly and for ever vindicated. Thus we see that the word of God, applied to the conscience by the Holy Ghost, is the great and sole agency employed by God for the regeneration and salvation of man. In many ways that word may be brought before us; we may read it for ourselves, or faithful men may declare it in our ears, but in whatever way it reaches us, it is only the entrance of

God's word that giveth us light. It was for this reason that St. Paul exclaimed: "I am not ashamed of the Gospel of Christ, for it is THE POWER OF GOD UNTO SALVATION to every one that believeth." (Rom. i. 16.)

To be born therefore of WATER is to be born by the agency of GOD'S WORD. In further proof of this I may quote our Lord's language to His disciples: "Now ye are clean through the WORD which I have spoken unto you." (John xv. 3.) Christ's word (as water) had cleansed them, so that by it He tells them they had been made pure. St. Paul's teaching is to the same effect: "Husbands, love your wives, even as Christ also loved the Church, and gave Himself for it; that He might sanctify and cleanse it with the washing of water BY THE WORD." (Eph. v. 25, 26.) In this passage God's people are represented as being cleansed in the word of truth as in a sea, and thus made ready, as a chaste bride, for the coming of the Bridegroom.

As there are many who believe that by this word "water" we are to understand baptism, I wish now to say on what grounds I utterly dissent from such an interpretation.

First: *If water be explained here as being the literal water of baptism, all mention of the Redeemer's work in the regeneration of man is excluded from a sentence in which Christ is teaching what is the* VERY NATURE *of regeneration.*

Our Lord is speaking of the regeneration of man; He mentions two agents, water and the Spirit. Of these, one, the latter, we know to be the Holy Ghost, without whom man cannot possibly be regenerated; the other is water. Now, if this be interpreted as literal water, it would teach that man is regenerated by the Holy Ghost and the simple element of water, without any mention of the work of Christ. Irreconcilable with this is the fact that the Bible teems with statements to the effect that we have LIFE only from the Lord Jesus Christ. He Himself says: "I am the life." St. John adds: "He that hath the Son hath life, and he that hath not the Son of God hath not life." For this reason, as well as that already adduced, namely, that Christians are directly stated to be begotten through the Gospel, I deem it wholly improbable that our Lord ascribes our regeneration here only to the Holy Ghost and literal water.

Secondly: *It is according to analogy, or what we know of other parts of Scripture, to believe that water is here mentioned as a* TYPE *of something deeper, and therefore not to be taken in its literal signification.*

In explaining the words, "Except a man be born of water," many urge that the word "water" must be understood in its absolutely literal sense, and affirm that no other interpretation is reasonable. In reply, I may say, there is no word of more varied significance in the whole Bible, than this word "water." For example, in this same Gospel we have no less than three distinct occurrences of the word water, and in each place a totally different signification is evidently demanded. The passages I refer to are the following: Chap. iii. 5,—the text in question; Chap. iv. 13, 14; and Chap. vii. 37, 38, 39. Now let it be granted for argument's sake, that when our Lord spoke to Nicodemus He meant literal water, it follows that when He addressed the woman at the well He meant literal water also, and would have her understand that, instead of water from *that* well, He would give her the water of Baptism, and Baptism would be in her a well of water springing up into everlasting life. Now, no one seriously believes such to be the true interpretation of the passage, as it is abundantly evident that our Lord designed to impress upon her mind a deep, life-giving truth, but which she, on her part, utterly failed to comprehend. By water, our Lord means here eternal life, and every other spiritual blessing which comes to us through Him. The " gift of God," says the Apostle Paul, " is eternal life in Christ Jesus our Lord," (Rom. vi. 23.) and therefore this living water is not *material* water, but eternal life, and every other holy gift, in Jesus Christ our Saviour. If now we turn to the seventh chapter of St. John, we find our Lord again speaking of water—" living water." Here, however, we have positive inspiration to tell us what He meant: " But this spake He of the Spirit, which they that believe on Him should receive." Thus water here means the Holy Ghost; but it had not this signification in the third chapter, for our Lord would not say: Except a man be born of the Spirit, and *of the Spirit;* water *there* must mean something else, and as I have already dwelt on its signification in the fourth chapter, it follows that we have the word water used in three different meanings in the third, fourth and seventh chapters of St. John. That water is thus variously to be explained, admits of no doubt, and therefore we may the more readily see its force in the passage before us, as indicating that great element by which God quickens the spiritually dead, namely, His Word.

Thirdly: *If by water were meant Christian Baptism, the Old Testament saints lacked the main element in regeneration, for they were never baptized.*

Baptism is essentially a New Testament ordinance, and therefore if our Lord were stating something absolutely new, we can hardly understand His surprise at the ignorance of Nicodemus. "Art thou," He said, "a master of Israel, and knowest not these things?" Nicodemus may have seen proselytes baptized, but neither he nor his fathers had ever seen that ordinance administered to one born in the faith of Israel. Indeed, if we insist that water here can only mean Christian baptism, we must exclude apparently from regeneration, and therefore from salvation, all those Old Testament saints whose rest, we know, is secured; all children dying unbaptized; all who at their last moments may be utterly unable to obtain baptism; even the very thief to whom our Lord on the Cross said: "This day shalt thou be with me in Paradise," besides hosts of others who for doctrinal reasons have not received this rite.

Fourthly: *If Baptism were God's great way of regenerating men, it is utterly beyond the power of any one to explain certain passages and facts of Scripture.*

St. Paul, for instance, says: " I thank God that I baptized none of you, but Crispus and Gaius; * * * for Christ sent me NOT TO BAPTIZE, but to PREACH THE GOSPEL." (1 Cor. i. 17.) Now such language is utterly inexplicable, if the water of baptism were the great means of regenerating men. Surely the great Apostle would hardly thank God he had had no part in the work of saving the

Corinthians, and surely Christ Himself would not have sent His servant to do the *less* and omit the *greater* work.

We now come to the examination of the second clause,

Born of the Spirit.

In nothing is Scripture clearer than in its testimony concerning the utterly lost condition of him who is yet in his sins, that is, the unregenerate man. Such an one, it declares, is a criminal on whose head *abides* the wrath of God. Having refused the salvation which is in Christ, and the blood which cleanseth from sin, his guilt is ever before God; it rises up like a cloud, calling for judgment, and therefore while he is in this state — separate from Christ through unbelief and impenitency of heart — emphatically it declares he shall not SEE life, but that the wrath of God ABIDETH on him. Far otherwise, however, is it with him who has fled for refuge to lay hold upon the hope set before us in the Gospel. Such an one stands JUSTIFIED from all things; his glorious substitute, the Lamb of God, has borne his sins and taken his place in wrath; the penalty of death, justly due his guilt, has been endured by Christ; and this sacrifice of the Son of God, having been accepted by the Father as the full and eternal satisfaction for all his sins, he stands absolutely FREE, UNCHARGED WITH FAULT BEFORE GOD. But this is not all. Not only is the believer forever delivered from death by virtue of the sacrifice of his chosen Substitute, but this same Substitute, even Jesus Christ, is made unto him an everlasting RIGHTEOUSNESS. As therefore the righteousness of Christ is of infinite merit by reason both of the dignity of His person and the perfection of His obedience, it follows that as *Christ* is precious, so is the *believer* precious to the Father. Thus, accepted in the Beloved, he stands wholly in the infinite righteousness of Another. For him Christ died, and for him wrought out while on earth a righteousness so perfect and sublime that even the awful holiness of the Father could *rest* in it as absolutely without fault.

Such then—the infinite merit of Christ—constitutes the ONLY RIGHT of the believer to stand before God and say: "I know Thou hast forever saved me. This is my only plea, as a child of God, and an heir of glory." So much then for his *right* to call God his Father in Christ, and to rest in that peace which comes from being justified by faith. His acceptance, his whole standing, rests entirely on the Lord Jesus Christ.

We now proceed to another and equally momentous question, namely,

What DISPOSITION is that, in the believer, by which, with the aid of the Holy Spirit, he is enabled to serve God?

Certainly he has none in his own natural heart, that being "deceitful above all things and desperately wicked." "It is not subject to the law of God, NEITHER INDEED CAN BE." In the emphatic language of St. Paul, the mind of the flesh, that is, the natural heart, is DEATH. Now, can the reader for one moment imagine that with such a heart *any* man can serve God? Sooner will water help fire to burn brighter, than our natural heart minister to the service of God. Observe, it is not *inability* to keep abreast of God's law to which I allude. It is not as if I said: As well might an eagle race with the lightning as our natural heart keep up to the perfect law of God; for in that case, the eagle might fly very swiftly, though unsuccessfully. There would be *failure* but not *antagonism*. With our natural heart it is far otherwise, "it is not subject to the law of God, neither indeed *can* be." To trust in this heart—to believe that it either can or will serve God—is like letting loose a wild zebra of the desert, in the fond hope that afterwards it will return at your call. It cannot possibly do so; its whole nature revolts against the yoke; it hates all restraint, and like the winds, it must be free.

Two mistakes in connection with this truth are very common; they are the following:—

First: *Many imagine that on their believing, God will change this natural, evil heart, and make it holy and good; while, secondly, others suppose the natural heart will be wholly done away with, so that it will not even exist.*

Now, with regard to the first of these errors, nothing is clearer than that God does not CHANGE the natural heart into that which is good and holy. Throughout the whole range of Scripture we do not once find the expression "change of heart." God does no mending, no re-furbishing; He CREATES ANEW. What therefore we do find in the word of God is, the doctrine of a new heart, and of a new spirit. Thus in Ezekiel, God says: "A *new* heart also will I give you, and a *new* spirit will I put within you; and I will *take away* the stony heart out of your flesh, and I will give you an heart of flesh." (xxxvi. 26.) So too St. Paul says: "Therefore, if any man be in Christ, he is a NEW CREATURE: old things are passed away; behold, all things are become new." (2 Cor. v. 17.) And again: "For in Christ Jesus neither circumcision availeth anything, nor uncircumcision, but a NEW CREATURE." (Gal. vi. 15.) "For we," that is, believers, "are His workmanship, CREATED IN CHRIST JESUS." (Eph. ii, 10.) Thus we see that Christ comes into the heart with this decree: "Behold, I make all things NEW." (Rev. xxi. 5.) The old heart, therefore, will not be re-made, or changed; on the contrary, it will continue till the end the same utterly hostile and corrupt nature that it was at first. But this, dear reader, will God do for you, should you now accept the Lord Jesus Christ, "A new heart also will He give you, and a new Spirit will He put within you."

The *second* error is refuted by the constant statement of the Apostles, as well as by the bitter experience of God's people in all ages, and in all lands. Who can read the epistles of St. Paul without seeing how terribly he had to struggle with an evil heart within? "I know," he says, "that in me (that is, in my flesh,) dwelleth NO GOOD THING." (Rom. vii. 18.) "I find," he adds, "a law, that when I would do good, *evil is present with me.* For I delight in the law of God after the inward man; but I see another law IN MY MEMBERS, warring against the law of my mind, and bringing me into captivity to the LAW OF SIN which is in my members. O wretched man that I am! who shall deliver me from the body of this death? I thank God through Jesus Christ our Lord." In a remarkable passage in Galatians, the same Apostle declares: "The flesh LUSTETH AGAINST THE SPIRIT, and the

Spirit against the flesh: and these are contrary the one to the other: so that ye may not do the things ye may wish." (Chap. v. 17, Ellicott.) These texts I quote, and many more might be added, only to show how desperately opposed to God's grace the natural heart is; for we see that even after a man has been saved by grace, it remains the same in its ineradicable hostility to God. It is true, we shall hereafter be wholly free from its contaminating presence when we stand with Christ in glory; true, that even here, by virtue of our union with the risen Redeemer, we are *legally* free from its DOMINION, and may *actually* be so from its BONDAGE, but we are in this life never free from its conscious presence; never free from the absolute necessity of our watching, waiting, praying, lest the flesh betray us into sin.

And now, by way of illustration, let us suppose the case of a man who, through grace, has believed on the Lord Jesus Christ. What is his position? The blood of Christ has availed to wash his sins forever away; but is this all? Suppose God were now to leave him, would he not soon be as deep in the mire as ever? Certainly, only lower down still. You want a servant; under the hope of reward, a savage offers himself; you accept his terms and he enters your service. In an unguarded moment he attacks you, and having robbed you of all your effects, leaves you for dead. On your recovery you send for him, pardon all his brutality, and inform him you freely forgive his outrage. Now, what have you done? Have you bettered the savage? No, not in the least. He was a savage *before* you forgave him, and he is a savage *after* you have forgiven him. He needs *more* than forgiveness; he needs to be made NEW; he needs A NEW HEART. Now Scripture discloses the great truth that God will forgive his sins; He will CREATE in him a NEW HEART, that is, he will absolutely call into existence that which before was not in him, and this He will do by the operation of the Holy Spirit. As this "new heart" is commonly known in Scripture by the name of the "*new man*," or other kindred terms, I shall henceforth speak of this new creation under this title, but before I proceed to explain the nature of the "new man," I wish again to call your attention to two truths which should ever be kept clear and distinct in our minds:—

First, our RIGHT to stand before God as accepted, lies wholly in the infinite merit of the Lord Jesus Christ; and secondly, our ABILITY to render God service lies in the *creation* within us of the "new man," together with the gift of the Holy Ghost.

The New Man.

Writing to the Romans, the Apostle refers to a great truth which, he says, they knew. This truth, which is of the greatest importance to us, is as follows: "Knowing this, that our *old man* was crucified with Him in order that the body of sin might be rendered powerless, that we should no longer serve sin." (Rom. vi. 6, Alford.) Now, here the Apostle speaks of some one in us under the title of "OUR OLD MAN," and the question arises to whom does he refer? The answer is immediately found by appealing to his Epistle to the Galatians, in which he says: "I have been crucified with Christ (co-crucified); it is, however, no longer I that live, but Christ liveth in me." (Chap. ii. 20, Ellicott.) In comparing these two passages we find that the "I" of Galatians stands for the "old man" of Romans; in other words, the "I" represents all the Apostle was by nature, as opposed to what he was by grace. The "I" was the "old man" in him: but this "I"—this "old man"—he declares, was crucified with Christ; that is, in the death of Christ, not only did God provide a full and ample satisfaction for the actual sins of His believing people, but He *then* and *there* condemned sin in the flesh, that is to say, God at that time passed judicial sentence of death upon our corrupt and fallen nature, so that it is NOW, like a man who has been tried, found guilty and condemned to die, legally, though not actually, DEAD. And *actually dead* it will be when God executes His sentence upon it by either the coming of Christ, or the personal removal of His people. And what was true in the case of St. Paul is affirmable of all believers, for of the whole family of faith it is said: "But they who are of Christ Jesus CRUCIFIED the flesh, with its passions and with its desires." (Gal. v. 24, Alford.) They all died with Christ; they all had the sin which is in their flesh, that is, their "old man," condemned; they all have been set free in the liberty which is in Christ Jesus.

We now come to the "NEW MAN," who, by the Holy Ghost, has been CREATED in the believer in righteousness and true holiness.

St. Paul, writing to the Ephesians, tells them that when they believed on the Lord, they did, at that moment, put *off* the old man and put *on* the "new." In pressing this vital truth upon them, his language is very strong, as he is most anxious they should walk worthy of their risen Lord. "But ye did not so learn Christ; if indeed ye heard Him, and were taught in Him, as is truth in Jesus, namely, that ye put off as concerns the former conversation the old man, which is being corrupted according to the lusts of deceit, and that ye are renewed in the spirit of your minds, and that ye put on THE NEW MAN WHICH WAS CREATED AFTER GOD IN RIGHTEOUS-

NESS AND HOLINESS OF TRUTH." (Eph. iv. 20-24, Rev. Trans.) Exactly similar to this is the statement in Colossians: "Do not lie one to another, seeing that ye have PUT OFF from you THE OLD MAN with his deeds; and have PUT ON THE NEW MAN, which is being renewed unto knowledge after the image of HIM THAT CREATED HIM." (Chap. iii. 9, 10, Ellicott.) So too in another passage, where the Apostle is showing how Christ had made both Jewish and Gentile believers new creatures in Himself, he says: "For He (Christ) is our peace, who made both (Jew and Gentile) one, and threw down the middle wall of the fence, (the whole ceremonial law which separated the Jew from the Gentile, but above all the *enmity* which separated both from God) to wit, the enmity, in His flesh; abolishing the law of the commandments in ordinances; that He might MAKE (lit. CREATE) the two into ONE NEW MAN in Himself, so making peace." (Eph. ii. 14, 15, Alford.) The "new man" here is not merely one who does not stand on national privileges, but one who has spiritually been made new by the Holy Ghost having created in him a new heart, called by the Apostle Paul THE NEW MAN. In writing to the Corinthians, the same inspired writer says: "Wherefore if any man be in Christ, HE IS A NEW CREATURE." (2 Cor. v. 17.) Not a *reformed* man, but a *new* man, "God's workmanship, CREATED IN CHRIST JESUS unto good works." (Eph. ii. 10.) And he is this new creature by virtue of God having created in him that which before he possessed not, namely, a heart to love and serve Him; a heart which from the very fact of its having been created "in righteousness and holiness of the truth," enables the believer, through the mighty and ever present help of the Holy Ghost, to walk in the light as Christ is in the light. And this walking in the light is no mere mechanical imitation of Christ, but the result of the Holy Ghost having begotten us anew in Christ Jesus. The promises which had gone before were all to the same effect; for God, speaking to Israel through Ezekiel, says: "A NEW HEART also will I give you, and a NEW SPIRIT will I put within you;" and in Jeremiah:

"But this shall be the covenant that I will make with the house of Israel; after those days, saith the Lord, I will put MY LAW IN THEIR INWARD PARTS, and WRITE IT IN THEIR HEARTS; and I will be their God, and they shall be my people. (Jer. xxxi. 33.)

Such, then, is the "new man" as described in Holy Scripture. In order, however, to make the whole clearer, I will ask you to observe three points:

First, The *origin* of its existence; secondly, the *time* when it occurs; and thirdly, the *result* of its being within us.

As regards the first, I have already shown it is of God, for the new man is said to have been created *after God* in righteousness and holiness of the truth. The Holy Ghost is that Person of the Trinity by whom this is effected, for our Lord distinctly states: "It is the spirit that quickeneth," (John vi. 63,) and that His people are all BORN OF THE SPIRIT. Life dwells in Christ. He is the life-giving one, and therefore he that hath the Son hath life; but this quickening power Christ has equally with the Father, for, "as the Father raiseth up the dead, and quickeneth them, even so the Son quickeneth whom He will." Still we are to understand that the Holy Ghost directly quickens the spiritually dead, for, in addition to what I have already quoted, St. Paul says: "The Spirit giveth life." (2 Cor. iii. 6.) And now let it be clearly understood that this everlasting life which we have in Christ Jesus is not that mere eternity of existence which the wicked will have in the "lake of fire;" *it is Christ in us* the hope of glory. The wicked *exist* here in this life without personal union with the Lord Jesus Christ, and they *shall so exist* throughout all eternity; they have existence, and that existence is eternal, but not LIFE ETERNAL, that is, LIFE IN CHRIST. This "life in Christ" God's people have; they have it from the time of their new birth, when the new heart was given them; and now that they have received it, though they are, like the wicked, still mortal as to their bodies, yet are they united for ever to Christ, and when He shall appear, they shall also appear with Him in glory.

Christ, therefore, the fountain, preserver and fulness of life, is the Author of *our* life: by His Holy Spirit He has quickened us, having created within us a new heart, which new heart is THE NEW MAN of which I have been speaking. To this new man, so created in us, the Holy Ghost testifies of Jesus Christ; fills with His glorious presence, strengthens, guides, directs, especially at a Throne of Grace, where, with groanings which cannot be uttered, he makes intercession with the saints, according to the will of God.

As therefore we have before seen that our RIGHT to stand before God in peace rests on the merit of ANOTHER, even on THE RIGHTEOUSNESS OF CHRIST, so now we see that our ABILITY to serve Him rests on the fact of there having been created within us a new heart in union with the will of God, with which new heart the Holy Ghost pleads, and, as being ever present with, strengthens, fills and guides.

Secondly, the time when this new creation takes place is that moment when the sinner first with the heart believes in Jesus Christ as his Saviour. As I shall treat of this subject in my third chapter, I must refer the reader to it for a full and definite declaration concerning that life which by faith is instantaneously communicated to the soul.

Thirdly, the results of the "new man" being within us are, that we are enabled, through the Holy Ghost assisting us, to walk with God and do His holy will. There is now within the believer that which really does love God, so that he can now say with the Apostle Paul: "I delight in the law of God after the inward man." He has indeed become a son, and as a son can glorify the Father through the Lord Jesus Christ. Ignorance of this truth leads to the most deplorable results, for it induces people to make a fond effort to try and serve God with a heart deceitful above all things, and desperately wicked. Not having received Christ by faith into their hearts, and therefore not having been born of the Spirit, they have only resident within them a principle which is in direct and incessant antagonism to God. The effort consequently to "make all things new," can only have one result, and that is, utter failure. How often, for instance, have poor drunkards come to the writer, burning with indignation against themselves on account of the degradation into which their own sins and follies had involved them. They have vowed and vowed again to leave all the past behind them; to give up sin in every form; to become entirely new, and henceforth only to soar upward to the skies. Their abhorrence of sin has been real; their intention to reform sincere; their prayers earnest, sometimes agonizing; but within a month they have gone back like a dog to its vomit and a sow that was washed to its wallowing in the mire. People have been in despair at the spectacle, but no other result could be looked for. Vehemency of desire and earnestness in vows will not take the place of the Lord Jesus Christ, and therefore, however much a poor drunkard may desire to reform, until he receives Christ by faith into his heart he is on the sand, and the house of fond expectations and visionary delights built thereon must inevitably fall. It is true indeed, men may sometimes give up drinking without becom in true Christians, but this is only reform, not salvation; and it is of salvation that I speak. No, the drunkard, as well as every other unsaved sinner, needs to be CREATED ANEW in Christ Jesus, and until he is, he must of necessity be the sport and prey of his own passions. I do not mean to deny that open violators of God's laws may not under certain circumstances effect an external reformation of their lives, a reformation, too, in every way to be desired as rendering them better able to understand the words of life spoken to them; but to serve as *sons* in God's house, never. Even the effort at external reformation is often futile, and this because these victims of passion trust in a heart which is not subject to the law of God, neither indeed can be; they trust in their indignation against sin; in their vehement desires; in the vows they are taking; in the strength which they imagine they possess; in everything, in fact, except in that which alone would save them, namely, the merits of the Lord Jesus Christ. Instead of trusting on Him who is mighty to save, they trust on their own hearts; and "he that trusteth in his own heart," Solomon says, "is a fool."

No, God's plan is wholly different: it is for the lost sinner to look to the Lord Jesus Christ, believe and live for ever; then at this moment of his believing is there created within him a new heart, one that DELIGHTS in the law of God, and though it has still to wrestle with the old and carnal nature, yet being ever aided by the Holy Ghost, it continually presses towards the mark for the prize of its high calling in Christ Jesus. It hates sin and loathes the garments spotted by the flesh; and, being GOD'S WORKMANSHIP, created in Christ Jesus unto good works, it knows God and is known of Him.

Chapter III.

Regeneration in its connection with Christ on the Cross.

WHEN our Lord said to Nicodemus: "Except a man be born of water and of the Spirit, he cannot enter into the Kingdom of God," the learned Jew was still as utterly unable to comprehend His meaning as before, and could only, in his astonishment, utter the unbelieving exclamation: "How can these things be?" On this Christ said: "Art thou a (the) master of Israel, and knowest not these things?" Evidently our Lord considered Nicodemus ought to have been familiar with these truths, as they were not new revelations but clear and blessed statements prophesied of in the old Testament Scriptures. Still, being Himself a merciful High Priest who always had compassion on the ignorant and on them that are out of the way, He proceeds to show Nicodemus, by referring him to a well known historical incident, that this great doctrine of the new birth, or regeneration through the uplifted Christ, was typically made known to Israel as far back as the days of Moses. This He does by referring him to the following event, recorded in the twenty-first chapter of the Book of Numbers: "And the people spake against God, and against Moses, wherefore have ye brought us up out of Egypt to die in the wilderness? for there is no bread, neither is there any water; and our soul loatheth this light bread. And the Lord sent fiery serpents among the people, and they bit the people; and much people of Israel died. Therefore the people came to Moses, and said, We have sinned, for we have spoken against the Lord, and against thee; pray unto the Lord, that He take away the serpents from us. And Moses prayed for the people. And the Lord said unto Moses, Make thee a fiery serpent, and set it upon a pole: and it shall come to pass, that every one that is bitten, when he looketh upon it, shall live. And Moses made a serpent of brass, and put it upon a pole, and it came to pass, that if a serpent had bitten any man, WHEN HE BEHELD THE SERPENT OF BRASS, HE LIVED." This was a scene in the history of Israel with which Nicodemus could not be but familiar, and therefore, with peculiar propriety, pointing him to that grand historical scene, Christ says: " As Moses lifted up the serpent in the wilderness, EVEN SO must the Son of Man be lifted up: that whosoever believeth in Him should not perish, but have eternal life." Now, here our Lord states two most important facts; *first*, that the uplifting of the brazen serpent in the wilderness was a type of Himself upon the Cross: and, *secondly*, that the physical results flowing to the bitten Israelites from a look at the serpent of brass were typical of the spiritual and eternal results which flow to our souls from a believing look at Him as the Bearer on the Cross of our appointed doom. The " even so" marks the exactness of the similitude. It follows, therefore, that any preaching which makes salvation less FREE, less EASY, less PERFECT, or less IMMEDI-

ATE than the healing effected by the type, is not the teaching of the Lord Jesus Christ.

What Nicodemus was anxious to know was, how a man could be born when he was old? Our Lord said it was by faith in Himself as uplifted on the Cross. Standing before this tremendous sacrifice, and believing on Christ thus offered, the sinner not only obtains the full and eternal pardon of his sins, but also full spiritual health, that is, he is BORN AGAIN, a new heart being given him and a new spirit put within him. Thus we see Christ has forever connected regeneration with faith in Himself as God's appointed sacrifice for sin; and so close and so real is this connection, that whenever a sinner believes in Jesus Christ as the bearer away of his sins on the Cross, at that moment is he also born again: at that moment he receives power—to use the language of St. John—to become a *son* of God.

As our Lord presses upon us the exactness of the similitude between the healing by the brazen serpent, and regeneration through faith in Himself as offered upon the Cross,

I shall now endeavour to point out some striking features in this resemblance.

First: *The people for whom the brazen serpent was uplifted in the wilderness were those dying absolutely without hope, and those for whom Christ died were the LOST.*

The Israelites who had been bitten had to die; no physician could heal them, no human arm could help them; the bite was certain death. For such the serpent of brass was lifted up, and for such alone. So Christ was lifted up for a certain object—TO SAVE THE LOST. If, therefore, there are any people in this world who are not lost—lost, I mean, in the sense in which Christ uses the word—then Christ did not die for them, for, in fact, they need no Saviour; but as the Scripture says positively that no such people exist, but that all have sinned and come short of the glory of God, it follows there is no man who may not be saved through faith in the Lord Jesus Christ, as all come under the title of THE LOST.

And now, dear reader, do you know what Christ means when He says you are lost? If you are not yet "in Him," and therefore forever free from all condemnation, I am very certain you do not; for no one grasps this awful fact by intuition, no one learns it by mere feeling, it can only come to our mind by the revelation of God's word. I will not therefore ask you whether you *feel* you are lost, or whether you *think* you are lost, but reverently and prayerfully to consider the fact that man's utterly LOST condition does not rest on theory, but on three very startling and most plainly revealed truths:—

(1.) On the imputation of Adam's sin, by which DEATH passed through unto ALL MEN, on the ground that ALL SINNED;

(2.) On the consequent depravation of our nature by which we inherit, as springing from Adam and standing in his guilt, a heart, or mind of the flesh, which is not subject to the law of God, neither indeed can be; and

(3.) On the ground of our daily wilful and repeated transgressions, by which, as sinning against light and truth, we are continually increasing our guilt.

And now as regards the first of these, namely, the imputation of Adam's sin, let us see on what ground it rests. The place in which this truth is most emphatically laid down is in the fifth chapter of Romans, where the following declaration is made on the subject: "For this cause, as by ONE MAN sin entered into the world, and by sin, death, and so DEATH PASSED THROUGH UNTO ALL MEN, for that (on the ground that) ALL SINNED. (Ellicott.) Now, here is a very forcible statement to the effect that Adam was our representative, and that WE SINNED in HIS SIN. St. Paul says: "By one man sin entered into the world." This is conceded by all. He affirms in the next place, "and by sin, death." This we know to be in accord with the terms of the original judgment: "In the day that thou eatest thereof thou shalt surely die." His third statement is a deduction or inference from the above: "And so death passed through (permeated) unto all men, on the ground that all sinned;" not "have sinned," but *sinned*, that is, in the act of Adam. Death is here represented as radiating or spreading out from a certain event, and that event was Adam's sin. But the question arises, Why was it thus? The answer is: On the ground that ALL SINNED. Not that each one of us is born an heir to immortal bliss, with an incorruptibility of body, and that this happy state exists until in an evil moment we sin and all is lost, but the awful sentence of death was passed upon all who should be born of Adam, ON THE GROUND that all sinned in him. The Apostle next proceeds to expand upon this truth, and adds: " For up to the time of the law there was sin in the world, but sin is not reckoned where the law is not. But death reigned from Adam to Moses, even over those who sinned not according to the similitude of the transgression of Adam, who is a figure (type) of the future (Adam)." The argument of the Apostle is as follows: He had just stated that death extended to all men on the ground that all sinned in Adam. He then goes on to say that, up to the giving of the law on Mount Sinai, sin was in the world, that is, there were bad passions everywhere shewing themselves in evil acts; but sin, he affirms, is not reckoned (set down as transgression) where there is no law. Notwithstanding all this—notwithstanding that God does not reckon that as sin which is done without the protest of His law — yet, nevertheless, DEATH REIGNED from Adam to Moses, even over those who had not sinned after the similitude of Adam's transgression. Now those who lived from Adam to Moses did not sin after the similitude of Adam's transgression. Adam had a well known and fixed law to live by. So also had Moses. Those who intervened had not; they had no revealed, declared law; they were, many of them, very grievous sinners, but they did not sin as Adam sinned, that is, against a known law; they followed the wild bent of their own vicious dispositions and knew no ruler but themselves. But God does not reckon as sin that which is done without the protest of law. Why, then, did death reign over them if sin was not reckoned to them? The answer is: BECAUSE THEY ALL SINNED IN ADAM. It is the same now; we have among us those who do not sin after the similitude of Adam's transgression, namely, infants and idiots; these do not, and cannot sin after the manner of Adam, that is, consciously, against a known law, yet death reigns over them. They sicken, suffer, languish, die; and people often ask, Why is this?—why do these poor unconscious ones, who have never committed actual sin, thus suffer? The answer is: Because they are resting under the imputation of Adam's guilt? They were born into the world with his sin upon them, and, as a consequence, his judgment, which is death. We know indeed from Scripture that such as die before they have become conscious agents will be saved through the merits of the Lord Jesus Christ; but then this does not alter the fact concerning the imputation of Adam's sin. The Holy Ghost in the word of God always places man under one or other of the following heads: The first man, Adam, or the second Adam—Christ. These constitute the only two camps in the world. All who have lived, or do live, or shall live, will be found in either one or other of these. Of those under the first Adam, Scripture affirms that they all die—die temporally, and die eternally. Of those under the second Adam, Christ, Scripture affirms that they have LIFE—life eternal; for though they, too, die temporally, yet in Christ they shall all be made alive. The passage I have quoted from Romans distinctly states three solemn facts: *first*, that sin entered into the world through the disobedience of Adam; *secondly*, that death was the consequence of that sin; *thirdly*, that all the human race is charged by God as having sinned in ADAM, and consequently the judgment of death which was pronounced on him, was pronounced upon the whole race as being in HIM. Dear reader, should you be in this great camp of sin, condemnation and death, your duty is to flee for your life from it, as Lot did from the gates of Sodom, for surely God has written it: "All in Adam die." Should any say, "How is this?" I answer, God is infinitely holy, infinitely just; what He ordains must be just—infinitely so. And let it be remembered that if God has ordained that Adam's guilt should be imputed to the human race, He has also ordained that Christ's righteousness shall be imputed to all who flee to His dear Son, though their sins be as red as scarlet and as deep as crimson die.

2.—Of the depravity of our natural heart, and its utter inability to serve God, I have already spoken at some length, and will now only add that this natural heart is the RESULT of our being born under condemnation, and comes to us by inheritance from Adam, in whom we have sinned. In other words, it is one of the terrible results which flow to us from that ONE SIN. Should we, however, fly to Christ, being then FREED from a state of condemnation, a new heart would be given us, even one created in righteousness and holiness of the truth.

3.—Under this head I wish to say a few words concerning God's holy law. *First*, it is "holy and just and good;" so searching and penetrating in its demands that it requires and will receive no other obedience than that which is absolutely and DIVINELY faultless. It not only says "Thou shalt NOT DO," but it states "This SHALT THOU BE." It not only utters the commandment "Thou shalt NOT steal," but it says "Thou SHALT love the Lord thy God with all thy heart." *Secondly*, such obedience as the Law requires no one has ever rendered except the Lord Jesus Christ, the "sinless one," in whom God was well pleased. *Thirdly*, the Law was not given to man as a means whereby he might obtain justification and pardon, but to reveal to him the awful heinousness of sin, and to show to him at all times what is God's standard of infinite holiness and right. St. Paul says distinctly: "By the Law is the KNOWLEDGE of sin." (Rom. iii. 20.) The Law is God's great metre for sin—His sin-ometre. Plunging this into the great river of humanity, and testing man by this holy and perfect standard, the reading is: "There is none righteous, NO, NOT ONE." (Rom. iii. 10.)

For these reasons, therefore, an unpardoned sinner must say: "I am lost—*first*, by the imputation of Adam's sin I am involved in the judgment of death; *secondly*, my own natural heart is enmity to God and utterly incapable of reformation; *thirdly*, every day I am increasing my guilt by wilful transgression, that is, by sin against light and truth. Being therefore CONDEMNED, INCAPABLE of REFORMATION, at least by any powers inherent in myself, and DAILY SINKING DEEPER INTO GUILT, I may well say I AM LOST."

Terrible, however, as is the condition of the sinner by nature, yet grace is ready to save him to the utmost. Just because man is by nature *lost*, therefore God has given His Son, that whosoever believeth in Him should not perish, but have everlasting life. If *sin* has abounded, *grace* has much more abounded, so that the imputation of Adam's guilt, with its consequent judgment of death, the inherent depravity of the natural heart, or the oft-recurring sins of daily life, are more than met by the transcendent salvation of the Son of God. The imputation of *Adam's guilt* is overbalanced by the imputation of *Christ's righteousness;* the depraved heart, by the creation of a new heart in righteousness and true holiness; and the recurring sins of daily life, by grace sufficient from on high. As God has thus made provision in Jesus Christ for the salvation of all, the sinner is without excuse. Down through all centuries of time come these glorious words, forever refuting the calumnies of men, of Satan, and of our own evil heart as to God's not wishing the salvation of the sinner, "And this is THE WILL OF HIM THAT SENT ME, THAT EVERY ONE WHICH SEETH THE SON and believeth on Him MAY HAVE EVERLASTING LIFE: and I will raise him up at the last day." (John vi. 40.) After such words, joy is for all, however burdened, who will accept the salvation of God. Hence arises a new condemnation, a condemnation only revealed by the Gospel, and expressed by Christ thus: "He that believeth not is condemned already, because he hath not believed in the name of the only begotten Son of God." And *this is the condemnation,* "that LIGHT is come into the world, and men loved darkness rather than light, because their deeds were evil." (John iii. 18, 19.) There is, in other words, no excuse; all MAY be saved who WILL. A man who will not receive Christ into his heart is like a patient in the hospital who refuses to take the physician's remedy. The physician says: "Your malady, if left to itself, will kill you, but take this, and you will undoubtedly recover." If he refuse, his death is his own fault; so is it with the sinner. It is true that he is in himself utterly lost, but Christ hastens to him, saying: I am come to SAVE THE LOST. If, therefore, the sinner finally rejects Christ, his doom is forever sealed, there remains no other sacrifice for sin.

Secondly: That which cured the Israelites was something OUTSIDE of themselves: they were to look AWAY from themselves at the brazen serpent; so, too, the sinner is not commanded to look at himself for healing, but to Christ on the Cross.

Most people look to the wrong place for salvation — to themselves rather than to Christ. I would class error here under two heads: *first*, those who cannot believe that Christ's death NOW avails for them, because they do not immediately see in themselves a holy and renewed life. Such people ignore the fact that this holy and renewed life can only be the RESULT of salvation by faith; it does not *go before*, it *follows after*. St. Paul, writing to the Ephesians, says: "In whom also *after that ye believed*, ye were sealed with that Holy Spirit of promise." The Holy Spirit came permanently to dwell in them AFTER they had believed in Christ. Let this be clearly borne in mind, for when men seek for rectitude of life they are only seeking that which in itself is most commendable. But the question is—How is it to be obtained? Let us suppose you have taken part in an unsuccessful rebellion. As a necessary result of your conduct your life is forfeit to the crown; to save yourself, you fly to a foreign country and there remain. At last, growing weary of exile, you say: "I would like to go back and live as a peaceable subject in my own land," but your friends warn you that it will be death for you to return until you can first have the ban removed. The crown has condemned you to death, and until that sentence has been revoked you cannot possibly return. First have the ban cancelled, and then return. So is it with the soul. "He that believeth not the Son shall not see life; but the **WRATH OF GOD ABIDETH ON**

HIM." (John iii. 36.) This is God's sentence on all out of Christ. You ask for rectitude of life; this is well, but before you can obtain grace to walk acceptably with God you must first have this awful sentence of wrath removed, and this most certainly will be the case when, as an utterly lost sinner, you look away to Christ and believe on Him as God's propitiation for your sins. *Secondly*, those who say that, because they cannot *feel* the truth of the Gospel in their heart, therefore they cannot accept it. This is like a man with small-pox saying he does not feel strong and well, and therefore refuses to take the doctor's medicine. The man *is* sick and cannot possibly *feel* anything else than sick; and the soul which is under the wrath of God cannot possibly feel the peace of acceptance in the Beloved when that peace has not yet been secured. Therefore God does not ask you to look *in* for feeling, but *out* of you to Christ for salvation. Salvation in Scripture is never once made to rest on *feeling* but on the finished work of Christ alone; and that this glorious work of Christ saves us we KNOW by virtue of God's written word. Christ says to you: "Verily, verily, I say unto you, he that believeth on Me HATH everlasting life." When, therefore, you believe on Him as one who has saved you by His death, you clearly know you *are* saved, simply because His word says so. There may be at first but little joy, or, on the contrary, there may be much. A great deal will depend both on temperament and on the appreciation which a man has of the gift he has just obtained. What is PROMISED to every soul who believes in Jesus Christ, is everlasting life. When once he is saved he is COMMANDED to rejoice.

Thirdly: There was life in a look at the brazen serpent: there is ETERNAL life in looking unto Christ.

The bitten Israelite lay dying in the dust; his flesh is swollen, his skin turned black; his tongue parched with thirst; life fast ebbing from him. Suddenly the cry is heard, "Look, and live." Where? he asks, where? They point him to the brazen serpent as it glitters in the sunlight, and say, "There!" In an instant his fading sight is turned toward it, and with a rush, the warm, healthy life-blood mantles to his cheek, the poison vanishes, he knows not where, and to his feet he springs rescued from the very jaws of death. So is it with the lost soul who looks to Christ; salvation comes to him in the look. The bitten Israelite could not possibly help himself, every moment the poison spread further and death came nearer. The physician could not heal him; no medicine, no burning, no amputation could arrest its terrible progress, or keep back the approach of death. God alone could help him; and God *did* help him, and by this typical serpent save him. Now our Lord says this brazen serpent was an exact representation of the way in which He saves and regenerates the soul. I suppose you, dear reader, to be one who has not yet been saved. You need the pardon of your sins—eternal life, the new birth, in fact, everything. Like the dying Israelite, you are utterly unable to save yourself, and therefore, just because of this utter helplessness—this extremity of misery and woe—God has exalted His Son Jesus Christ to give you salvation to the uttermost and to place you as an heir in the kingdom of His glory. Pointing you, therefore, to Christ on the Cross as His eternal satisfaction for sin, and knowing all your need, He says: "Behold the Lamb of God," LOOK UNTO HIM AND LIVE. Complete *healing* came to the Israelite from looking to the serpent: infinite *salvation* will come to you from looking to Christ. By this I mean that look of faith which, on the authority of Holy Writ, sees in Christ on the Cross infinite satisfaction for all your sins—instantaneous life for your soul. And now, just to make this glorious truth clearer to you, I will state two things of great importance: *Why* you should look to Christ, and *how* you should look. First, because, in the death of our Lord, an infinite satisfaction was made for all your sins. Sin demands punishment. The law of God, holy, just and good, cries out for vengeance on all who break its precepts. You have broken them times without number, and therefore your life is forfeit to the law. How, then, will you be freed from your sins? The Scripture says: "Without shedding of blood is NO REMISSION;"

(Heb. ix. 22) and the blood which alone remits is the BLOOD OF CHRIST. Here then, on the Cross, Christ bore to the full all the sins of those who had believed or should in after ages believe on Him. Here too, on this same Cross, for their healing was He wounded. Isaiah sums it all up in two sublime verses: " All we, like sheep, have gone astray; we have turned every one to his own way, and the Lord hath LAID ON HIM the iniquity of us all." It was therefore God who laid our sins on Christ, and burdened Him with the weight of our iniquities. In the fifth verse we have given us the reason of Christ's death on the Cross: "He was wounded for *our* trangressions, He was bruised for *our* iniquities, the chastisement of *our* peace was upon Him; and with HIS STRIPES WE ARE HEALED." (Is. liii. 5, 6.) On the Cross, therefore, our glorious Redeemer presented His *own* righteousness for acceptance, and *our sins* for punishment; and God the Father accepted this awful death as the eternal propitiation, or satisfaction, not only for the sins of His *own* people, but also for the sins of THE WHOLE

WORLD. (1 John ii. 2.) "Christ, by the grace of God, tasted death FOR EVERY MAN," (Heb. ii. 9,) and therefore there was no one who ever *did* live, or no one who ever *shall* live, for whom Christ did not die. Look then, dear reader, to Him. Here in Christ's DEATH is God's satisfaction for all your sins. He will, according to His own word, accept this death as the full remission of all your guilt, as your title to sonship, and inheritance to glory, provided only this day you thus accept Him by faith. Secondly, *how* you are to accept Him : by simple faith, "For by grace are ye saved THROUGH FAITH," nothing more. You wish to draw nigh to God. Scripture says you may assuredly do so through Jesus Christ. Before you now, He stands the Lamb of God for sinners slain. God asks you simply to believe on Him and live for ever. Can you not therefore say : O Lord, I do from my heart *believe* that Thou by this thine awful death dost NOW SAVE ME FROM DEATH, and that Thy perfect righteousness is accepted by the Father for me; and with my mouth I do *confess* that

Thou art my Saviour, who hast redeemed me with Thy precious blood, whereof the Father hath given proof in that He raised thee from the dead. This is Scriptural faith, and this is all God asks of you in order to be saved. It is not therefore faith *in yourself*, faith in your resolutions of amendment, faith in any effort you may make, but faith in Christ—in His work—in His word. God will not save you for what *you* are, but for what *Christ* is, and therefore the Holy Ghost asks you to look with faith to Christ on the Cross and with the whole heart believe that there Christ tasted death FOR YOU.

And when, dear reader, you do so look, you will not only be eternally saved, but BORN AGAIN, that is, the Blood of the Lord Jesus will not only wash away your sins, and His righteousness be made the ground of your justification, but your soul will then be QUICKENED by the power of the Holy Ghost working in you through Jesus Christ. Nicodemus wished to know how a man could be born again. Our Lord brings back to his mind the grand old historical scene of the brazen serpent, and then tells him: "EVEN SO must the Son of Man be lifted up: that whosoever believeth in Him should not perish, but have eternal life." Now Christ has not only life in Himself, but He has power to quicken or give life to all who believe on Him. He is the "BREAD THAT GIVETH LIFE," and therefore whosoever believingly looks to Him, is at that instant, by Him, quickened into spiritual life. There is at that moment created within him the *new heart* of which Ezekiel speaks; the *new man* of whom St. Paul speaks; in other words, he is *born again*, and has undergone that great change without which no man can see the kingdom of God. Understand, therefore, that salvation is not merely the pardon of our sins, and the promise of infinite blessings in the future. It is far more: it is at once the eternal remission of our sins by virtue of the sacrifice of Christ—the being formally pronounced righteous by reason of the perfect obedience of Christ reckoned to us, and, at the same time, the creation within us of a new heart in righteousness and true holiness. This new and God-loving heart comes to us from Christ through the power of the Holy Ghost, and takes place whenever the sinner flies to Christ and believes on Him.

To conclude—This salvation is INSTANTANEOUS. The *instant* the dying Israelite looked to the brazen serpent he was made well; and the *instant* a sinner from the heart believes in Christ he is eternally saved. But many say: How is this possible?—has not *repentance* to come in first, and is not repentance deep and prolonged sorrow for sin?—if it be such, how can salvation by any possibility be instantaneous? In reply I must say, that, certainly, if by repentance were meant "deep and prolonged sorrow for sin," then the statement that salvation is a gift instantaneously conferred, could not be maintained; but that life is so conferred, is the emphatic teaching of our Lord in His conversation with Nicodemus, as well as in His repeated statements throughout the whole Gospel of St. John. The question then is, What is meant by repentance?

By repentance in Scripture is meant an *after mind* or *thought;* hence a *change of mind.* Thus Esau found no place of repentance, though he sought it carefully with tears. His anxiety was to induce his father to give him the blessing he had already bestowed on Jacob. This Isaac would not do, and Esau could not make him repent or *change his mind.* So too in the case of the two sons. (Mathew xxi. 28-32.) One son said I will not, but afterward he *repented* and went—that is, on reflection, he saw he had done wrongly, and this change of *mind* led him to change of *conduct.* Repentance is therefore not mere sorrow for sin; it is a change of mind leading to a change of conduct. Now the point I wish you especially to observe is this:—Repentance does not of itself and by itself mean sorrow. There may, or there may not be deep grief connected with repentance; all depends on God's individual dealing with the soul. In some instances there may be nothing experienced save unaffected *joy,* and in such cases the repentance is just as real, as true, and as much "unto life," as in those instances where there is nothing but the deepest grief. All I wish you to notice is—repentance does not of itself mean sorrow on the one hand, nor joy on the other, but that *change of mind* which leads to a total change of conduct. This will be seen more clearly if we consider the following facts:—

First, man's mind needs to be wholly changed. Man is by nature wholly wrong in all his ideas about God, about Satan, about the world, and even about himself. This is the result of the fall by which his mind has been made not only dark, but very darkness itself. "Ye were sometimes *darkness*," says St. Paul, in writing to the Ephesians, "but now are ye *light* in the Lord." The result of all ignorance is, that people believe the suggestions of Satan and the promptings of their own heart, and thus entertain a thousand wrong ideas about God and the way of salvation. What people therefore need is, to have God's glorious Gospel preached to them—that is, the revelation of His will, in order that they may see how wrong all their ideas are. When, then, a man on this representation of the truth changes his mind about God and His Son Jesus Christ, this is repentance toward God.

Take for instance the case of St. Peter's sermon on the day of Pentecost. When the Apostle had proved to them that they had been guilty of crucifying the Lord of life and glory, they were overwhelmed with grief; they cried out, "What must we do to be saved?" Now this deep sorrow and unfeigned remorse is just what many would call *repentance;* but the Apostle, so far from calling it repentance, says: "Repent and be baptized every one of you." What he meant to convey was that inasmuch as these people knew nothing of God as reconciled in Jesus Christ—nothing about salvation being wholly *completed* on the Cross—nothing, in fact, about God or about themselves—therefore they should immediately repent, that is, not give way to wild despair, or go about seeking to establish their own righteousness, but, on the representation of the Gospel, change their minds and see God as willing to receive them into favour through the merits of His dear Son.

Secondly, repentance is always in close connection with *faith;* that is, repentance towards God always occurs at the *same time* as faith in the Lord Jesus Christ. Every passage in the word of God in which salvation is said to be instantaneously conferred on him that believeth proves this. Take, for instance, the following passage: "The hour is coming, and now is, when the dead shall hear the voice of the Son of God, and they that hear shall live." Now, if repentance is to come in at all, and we know it is indispensable, it must come in between death and life; the dead are to *hear*, and when they hear they are to *live*. Nothing is mentioned but hearing, that is, with faith, for Christ says: "Verily, verily, I say unto you, he that BELIEVETH ON ME HATH EVERLASTING LIFE." It follows, therefore, that this hearing is believing, and that this believing must and does include REPENTANCE. St. Paul, however, distinctly tells us what repentance is, and when it occurs. Writing to Timothy, he tells him that "the servant of the Lord must in meekness instruct those who oppose themselves; if God, peradventure, will give them repentance *to the acknowledging of the truth.*" (2 Tim. ii. 25.) Here we see repentance is the acknowledging the truth as it is in Jesus, and so acknowledging it as to believe in it with the heart, and thus to be made new by its power.

Thirdly, Repentance is not always accompanied by sorrow. People say: Does not the Scripture affirm that "godly sorrow worketh repentance to salvation not to be repented of"? Certainly it does; and wherever God works deep grief in a man's soul for his sins, it is a blessed thing, for it will surely lead him to Christ. But God's ways are not uniform in dealing with the soul. On some minds the light gradually arises as a glorious truth filling the soul with joy unspeakable, and in this instance the repentance is just as deep, just as real, as in the case where there is the most unfeigned sorrow. Repentance is not joy or sorrow, it is that change of mind which leads to the acknowledgment of the truth. The Ethiopian did not understand the Prophet Isaiah; but Philip, having been taken up into his chariot, explains to him the salvation of Christ. On this the eunuch repents, that is, acknowledges to the full the truth he has heard, and joyfully believing in Christ, is immediately baptized. This was a change of mind to the acknowledgment of the truth, which is true repentance. It took place at the same time as when by faith he grasped Christ; for there can be no repentance towards God separate from faith in our Lord Jesus Christ.

How different is all this from what is generally advanced concerning repentance. According to the popular idea, repentance is a period of intense suffering on account of sin through which a man *must* pass before he can be saved; and furthermore, that this intense sorrow causes God's favour to shine upon us, and is in itself one of the main reasons why God pardons us. Now nothing could be more thoroughly destructive of the Gospel than this impression. It leads people to look *into themselves* for feelings rather than *up to Christ* for salvation; it drives them to despair on the one hand, or to utter indifference on the other; for, after seeking in vain for feelings which never can be in the fallen heart, unless God especially put them there, they give up all for lost. Others put off coming to Christ until some time when they hope to *feel* a sorrow for sin which they do not at the present. It inverts the whole order of God's economy as illustrated by the brazen serpent; for it makes a man to a very large extent his own healer rather than Christ, and thus turns away his eyes from that glorious Being whom God has exalted for our salvation. Understand, therefore, I do not depreciate sorrow; on the contrary, whenever it comes from God it works repentance unto salvation. So, too, does the " goodness of God" (Rom. ii. 4) effect the same. All I wish to say is: repentance is in itself neither joy nor sorrow. There may be, by God's ruling in individual cases, intense sorrow for sin, as the soul comes into the full and glorious light; or, there may be, on the other hand, intense joy; but, whether joy or sorrow, *repentance* takes place in both, and is as real in the one case as in the other. Repentance—to sum up all I have said—is that change of mind which takes place in every man who having had wrong ideas about God, about the redemption of Christ, about himself, is led, through the revelation of the Gospel to see his error and believe in Christ. Repentance, therefore, toward God is that *change of mind* which is *inseparably* connected with FAITH IN CHRIST, and is always followed by a change of life. What is the practical effect of all this? It is that the poor sinner can be saved—and God means that he should be saved—directly and instantaneously by the Saviour. God points you, dear reader, to the Lord Jesus Christ on the Cross, and says: LOOK, BELIEVE, AND LIVE. Should you ask: What am I to believe? I answer—That all that was necessary for your eternal redemption was FINISHED there; that *there* you see CHRIST TASTING DEATH FOR YOU, so that nothing remains but for you to receive salvation as a gift. Can you not NOW look up and live forever? believing that He by His death saves you from death, and that hereafter He will be your eternal Friend, your Saviour and your God. Hesitate not. Look not to your feelings, but up alone to this glorious Redeemer, and if this day you set to your seal that God is true by accepting Christ as THE ONE whose death and righteousness have procured your salvation, *this day*, God's word declares, will you pass from death unto life, and *this day* be written among the living.

I sometimes wonder how people can entertain doubts as to the ability of Christ to save them. It is like a man coming to a dead halt before London bridge: hundreds of heavy waggons laden with merchandise, beside carriages and foot passengers, are hurrying over, as they have for years gone by, and yet he stands afraid to trust himself upon the bridge. The policeman asks him to "move on," but he still hesitates, and tells him he fears the bridge will not bear him. "The man's mad." mutters the policeman, and leaves him to himself. And can *you* doubt, dear reader, the power of Christ's death to save *you* to the uttermost? Has not that blood saved Paul, the chiefest of sinners? Has it not washed away the defilement of all God's people? Has it not obtained peace for all God's waiting people? and have not all their burthens. their sins, their sorrows and their cares been fully borne by Him? And are YOU afraid to cast your weary heart, laden though it be with sins, upon Him, and believe that NOW His mighty sacrifice avails for your instantaneous salvation? Have you discovered faults in Him whom God has pronounced faultless? Or, does not that satisfy YOU which satisfied GOD? No, dear reader, hesitate not. Do not look into the *future*, and sadly hope that in some as yet unreached time God will make with you a treaty of peace; but, standing before the awful sacrifice of the death of Christ, believe that HERE thy soul finds life; that here CHRIST, by this tremendous death, FOR EVER PUTS AWAY THY SINS.

"Come, now, and let us reason together, saith the Lord: though your sins be as SCARLET, they shall be as WHITE AS SNOW; though they be RED LIKE CRIMSON, THEY shall be as WOOL." (Isaiah i. 18.)

CONCLUSION.

Looking unto Jesus; or, Growth in Grace.

FOR the comfort of those who have already looked believingly to Christ, I will now subjoin a few reflections on the mode in which we are to grow in grace.

First, by duly appreciating the sanctification ALREADY obtained for us, through the offering of the body of Jesus Christ, once for all.

The believer is the subject of *two* sanctifications; one, already and absolutely perfect; the other, progressive. The first is that sanctification which all believers have in virtue of their union with Christ, by which they are eternally set free from the dominion of sin, and made holy by the holiness of His blood. The second is that progressive work of the Holy Ghost in the heart by which the believer is daily brought into closer subjection to the will of God. Let us now briefly consider the first.

In the Epistle to the Hebrews there are three remarkable statements made about sanctification: first, that "both He that scantifieth and they who are scantified are all OF ONE." (Heb. ii. 11.) This implies the perfect and eternal union which exists between Christ and His people, as is clearly seen by referring to verse 14, which declares that as the *children* are partakers of flesh and blood, *He* also *Himself* likewise took part of the same. Secondly, that the sanctification of the believer was the result of the will of the Father, that is, according to His purposes in grace, and, furthermore, that this sanctification was effected through the offering of the body of Jesus Christ, once for all. The words of the text are as follows: "In which will we HAVE BEEN SANCTIFIED through the offering of the body of Jesus Christ, once for all." (Chap. x. 10, Alford.) Believers being, as we have just learned, one with Christ, rest forever in all the blessed and abiding consequences of that eternal offering by which He both washed away their sins and consecrated them to the service of God. By that offering they have *been* sanctified, that is, they have *been* once and forever WASHED; once and forever SEPARATED; once and forever CONSECRATED; and once and forever MADE HOLY by the sprinkling of Christ's blood. By the offering of the body of Jesus Christ the sanctification of the believer is absolutely complete, in that he occupies a place of holy separation from the service of sin, and stands now, as he shall alway stand, perfect in the righteousness of Christ, and holy with the holiness of that blood by which he is sprinkled. This truth is forcibly brought out in verse 14: "For by one offering He hath PERFECTED FOR EVER them who are sanctified." However poor and unworthy a believer may be in himself—and the more we grow in grace the more will the sense of our unworthiness crowd itself upon us—yet, as sanctified through the offering of the body of Jesus Christ, he is both beautiful and precious in the Father's sight. He is beautiful because Christ's righteousness covers him, and he is precious by virtue of that precious blood by which he is sprinkled; for by that one offering he has been perfected for ever.

The third statement in Hebrews concerning sanctification by Christ is as follows: "For the bodies of those beasts whose blood is brought into the sanctuary by the high priest for sin, are burned without the camp. Wherefore Jesus also, that he might sanctify the people with His own blood, suffered *without the gate*. Let us go forth therefore unto Him *without the camp*, bearing His reproach." (Chap. xiii. 11-13.) That is, Christ, in order that He might be a perfect sin-offering for His people, consented to suffer without the gate. He voluntarily took the place of shame and reproach by dying as one utterly rejected and cast out both by Israel and the Gentile world. He did it that He might sanctify His people with His own blood. Wherefore, urges the Apostle, let us go forth unto Him without the camp, bearing His reproach. The great lesson inculcated by this passage is the necessity of our co-suffering with Christ in separation from the world and in union with Him, for if we *suffer* with Him we shall be also glorified together. What then is meant by sanctification through the blood of Christ?

First, it means our title and right to stand evermore before God as *worshippers* in his spiritual temple. Sanctification is a word which belongs to *temple service*, in the same way that justification is a forensic or judicial word belonging to a court or judgment seat.

Secondly, it means that which was effected for us through the offering of the body of Jesus Christ, once for all.

Thirdly, the *time* when we are sanctified by the offering of the body of Jesus Christ, is that moment when we are justified by faith that is in Him. When therefore the Father pronounces a sinner JUST by virtue of the merits of Jesus Christ, reckoned to him, He also, at the same time, accepts him as once and forever SANCTIFIED by the offering of the same Saviour.

Fourthly, the sanctification of which I speak, namely, that effected through the offering of Jesus Christ, is one which is absolutely complete. St. Paul says: "In which will we *have been* sanctified," implying that this is not a sanctification which is in process of completion, but one which, inasmuch as it rests on the absolutely complete work of Christ, is in itself forever perfect. So too in Acts, St. Paul calls believers the "sanctified," (chap. xx. 32,) where the word implies those who have been sanctified. Our Lord also in sending the Apostle to the Gentiles, says: "That they may receive forgiveness of sins and inheritance among them which *are sanctified* by faith that is in Me." (Chap. xxvi. 18.) Furthermore, this sanctification is not only perfect, it is FOR EVER. The ancient temple service was one unending series of sacrifices and cleansing processes, for no sooner was a man legally cleansed than through some inadvertence he again incurred guilt, and therefore again needed ceremonial cleansing; but Christ being come, an high priest of good things to come, not by the blood of goats and calves, but by His own blood, entered once into the holy place, and therefore because that precious blood was all-availing—because nothing further remained to be done—the Apostle states that "by one offering He hath perfected FOR EVER them that are sanctified."

Fifthly, this sanctification by the blood of Christ implies our being MADE HOLY with that holiness wherewith Christ's blood is holy. It may not be possible to grasp all that this sanctification means, but we know what it *includes*. It includes our everlasting SEPARATION as a royal priesthood and a peculiar people, from the unholy dominion of the world, of Satan and of the flesh; our perpetual CONSECRATION in thought, word and act to the service of God and of His Christ; our indivisable and glorious UNION with Him who is the Resurrection and the Life; and finally our ADMISSION as those made holy by the sprinkled blood, into that spiritual, but still real temple, in which God's people forever celebrate His praise.

Seeing thefore that *in* the will of the Father, and *through* the offering of the body of Jesus Christ, we have been once and forever sanctified; seeing that by God's own hand we have been separated as an holy nation and consecrated as a royal priesthood to His service, how earnestly should we endeavour to illustrate by our daily walk and conversation the reality of this separation and the power of this consecration to God. Indeed this grasping through the Holy Spirit the full meaning of our complete sanctification by Christ, and then endeavouring through grace to walk conformably to our calling, is one of God's most blessed ways for stimulating our faith and quickening our zeal. Ignorance of God's will and of Christ's work must of necessity produce in us laxity in life, and therefore a deep and sanctified knowledge of this most glorious truth is not only important, it is vitally necessary for the development and perfection of the inner man; and, above all, for enabling us to fulfil the high and holy position we occupy as chosen witnesses of God.

As there is a *completed* sanctification effected for us through the offering of the body of Jesus Christ, once for all, so also is there a *progressive* sanctification wrought in us by the operation of the Holy Ghost. In considering this latter, I think it all important to note that whether we are considering justification or sanctification, God, in both cases, is always the giver and we only the receivers of blessing. When a sinner is rescued from death, the salvation by which God effects that deliverance is repeatedly declared to be God's GIFT: "The *wages* of sin is death, but the gift of God is eternal life through Jesus Christ our Lord." This truth, however, is most freely admitted by all who know the Gospel of God's grace, and therefore I need not further dwell on the subject; but the point I wish to enforce is this, that when we come to consider the great theme of our practical sanctification, we appear to ignore, or at least forget the fact that in this, as well as in justification, God is the bountiful giver and we only the receivers of blessing. The popular idea of sanctification is RENUNCIATION; in other words, that it consists in those acts of renunciation by which we GIVE UP anything which ministers to the flesh rather than to godly edifying. Now in this lies the mistake, for renunciation is the RESULT, not the principle of sanctification. The last invitation of the Bible to weary sinners is: "And whosoever will, let him TAKE the water of life freely." It is not earn or purchase, but take, as a free and royal gift from God. So, too, in practical sanctification, growth in grace is in proportion as we take or appropriate Christ to ourselves by faith, and renunciation is the *result* of this reception of Him into our hearts. The great principle in justification is, Believe and *live;* in sanctification, Believe and *grow.* In justification the sinner receives Christ into his heart as his life; in sanctification the saint receives the same Saviour as the mighty Conqueror, who is able to subdue all things to Himself. Christ is the portion of His people, and it is the exalted office of the Holy Spirit to make this glorious truth more clear and convincing to our minds. We see how nature acts. When winter reigns in all its icy power in our land, how can we escape its rigor? Can we with our own voice and will renounce it? Shall we break off the crisp icicles, cart away the snow, and call it summer? No, for it would be winter still. We must wait till the fiery sun comes back, and then its beams will warm the earth, unlock its frozen rivers, and make its death-like fields green again. The sun— nothing but the sun—will make the summer, and so is it with the soul. If the Christian has grown cold, and spiritual winter reigns within him, he needs indeed to renounce all the besetting sins and unholy influences which have impeded his course and checked the development of grace; but the only way in which this blessed result can be effected is by Christ afresh coming in as the Sun of righteousness and making summer in his soul. Not to heathen, dead in trespasses and sins, but to lapsed and lukewarm Christians did Christ utter these words: "Behold, I stand at the door and knock: if any man hear my voice and open the door, I will come in to him, and will sup with him, and he with Me." (Rev. iii. 20.) These Laodiceans were thus shown the remedy for their backslidden state; they were satisfied with winter in their hearts, and Christ wished to make summer there, therefore he stood at the door and knocked. So is it with us now. Christ having saved us by His blood from the judgment of offended Law, is now anxious to save us to the uttermost from the power of indwelling sin, from the snares of Satan and from the bondage of the world. Therefore He stands and knocks. You pray, and no doubt very earnestly, that you may be delivered from self; but self cannot cast out self. We must arise and open the door and let Christ in, and He will crowd out self. And here comes in the work of the Holy Spirit. How earnestly do we often pray that we may be filled with the Spirit, and when that prayer is being answered we realize it by His lifting up Christ within us— by Christ's *increasing*, and our *decreasing*. The Spirit does not speak of Himself but of Christ. "He shall testify of Me," were the words by which our Lord declared to His disciples the office of the Holy Ghost, and therefore we are ever to understand that the more we have of the Spirit, the more we realize that Christ dwells in our hearts by faith.

Three facts I would have the reader especially notice: *First*, In the economy of grace God designed that each one of His children should come into all the fullness of blessing in Christ Jesus. As God did not leave Israel after He had overthrown Pharaoh and his host in the Red Sea, but bade the nation rather press on and occupy the land of promise, so now, in dealing with us, He does not rest content with merely saving us from wrath, but urges us to go up at once and possess all the riches of that inheritance of glory we have in Jesus Christ. There are no poor in heaven, and God would have none in grace. Christ said to the wretched and miserable in Laodicea: "I counsel thee to buy of the gold tried in the fire, that thou mayest be RICH"; and St. Paul, in comforting the Philippians, says: "My God shall supply all your need according to His RICHES IN GLORY in Christ Jesus." So also in praying for the Ephesians he says: "For this cause I bow my knees unto the Father of our Lord Jesus Christ, that He would grant you according to the riches of His glory to be strengthened with might by His Spirit in the inner man; that Christ may dwell in your hearts by faith; that ye, being rooted and grounded in love, may be able to comprehend with all saints what is the breadth, and length, and depth and height; and to know the love of Christ, which passeth knowledge, THAT YE MIGHT BE FILLED WITH ALL THE FULLNESS OF GOD." Poverty therefore in grace is most inexcusable; it not only implies spiritual sloth on our part, but also contempt for the glorious and perfect inheritance we have in Christ. *Secondly*, All the riches of grace are summed up in Christ. " He is made unto us wisdom, and righteousness, and SANCTIFICATION and redemption," (1 Cor. i. 31,) " for in Him dwelleth all the fullness of the Godhead bodily." And " we are complete in Him which is the Head of all principality and power." *Thirdly*, Begin the day by giving thanks to God, which always causeth us to triumph in Christ Jesus. Let the first word your voice utters be thanksgiving—thanksgiving for future but still certain victory. Jacob feared his brother Esau, but his real wrestle was with the angel of the covenant. The battle was fought and the victory gained before he even saw his brother; and so with us in the spiritual contest, faith gains the victory before the battle of the day is fought. Before us is the world which lieth in wickedness; the devil going about as a roaring lion; and our own hearts, deceitful above all things and desperately wicked. These three, with the principalities and powers which come and go at the bidding of Satan, we have to meet. There is no possible escape, and therefore battle with them we must; the only question being, when the day with its fighting is over, shall we be lamenting a defeat suffered, or rejoicing in a victory gained? Surely we need not wait long for an answer; greater is He who is for us than all who are against us, and because this is the case, the victory may be fully decided before we, so to speak, meet our enemies face to face. Our greatest trouble is always with our own evil heart, for when we go to God in prayer, we too often stagger through unbelief, and fail to grasp the victory of faith. And here I wish to press upon the reader that the real contest is with *unbelief;* for when in prayer we have gained strength, simply to trust

Christ, then are we more than conquerors—then can we rest in peace. Now what is this trusting? It is believing that our prayer *is heard;* that Christ *will* dwell in our hearts; that His strength *will* be made perfect in our weakness, and that He Himself will subdue our enemies on every side. The prophet says: " Thou wilt keep him in perfect peace whose mind is stayed on Thee, because he TRUSTETH on Thee." And the child of God who has learned wholly to trust Christ, will not only grow like a cedar in Lebanon, but will rest in perfect peace when the whole world rocks beneath his feet. If any should ask how we are to obtain this faith? I answer, *first,* by a reverent and prayerful study of God's holy word; and *secondly,* by earnest continuance in prayer. The study of the Bible is absolutely necessary for our spiritual growth. It is the witness of the Holy Spirit to the truth as it is in Jesus, and therefore as one has well said: " To desire to know *more* than is written is presumption; to be contented with knowing *less,* is contemptuous; it is being satisfied that darkness should occupy a place only to be filled by light."

The following are three conditions of successful prayer: (1.) Abiding in Christ, and His word abiding in us. (John xv. 7.) (2.) The work of the two Intercessors, the Holy Ghost here on earth interceding *in* us, and Christ the Advocate on high interceding *for* us. (Rom. viii. 26, John xiv. 14.) (3.) Faith: "What things soever ye desire, when ye pray, BELIEVE that ye receive them, and YE SHALL HAVE THEM." (Mark xi. 24.)

The Holy Spirit is described in Scripture as the *Seal,* the *Unction* and the *Pledge.* He who seals us is God. St. Paul says: "Now He which stablisheth us with you in Christ, and hath anointed us, is God, who hath also sealed us, and given the earnest of the Spirit in our hearts." (2 Cor. i. 22.) The Spirit is therefore not the Sealer, but the Seal. He is God's Seal, and with Him the Father sealed His own Son, as we read in John, "For Him hath God the Father sealed," that is, by the descent of the Holy Ghost on the day of His baptism. As Christ Himself the Head was sealed, so are His people. And, be it observed, it is only *in* Him that they are so sealed, because it is only when divine love has brought us out of the place of wrath and put us in the place of abiding reconciliation, even in Christ, that the Holy Spirit can come down into our hearts as the heavenly seal of the Eternal Father. Therefore we read as follows: "In whom also after that ye believed ye were sealed with that Holy Spirit of promise, which is the earnest of our inheritance." (Eph. i. 13.) Now, the verb to seal has in Scripture three significations: 1st, to ratify or confirm; 2nd, to close up from sight, to keep in reservation; 3rd, to complete. God ratifies and confirms the everlasting salvation of those who have laid hold on His covenant of peace by sending to them the seal of His Spirit. As a man ratifies and confirms a document by affixing his seal, so when a sinner, on the credibility of God's word, has accepted Christ as the eternal ransom of his soul, God ratifies His word by sealing that man with the Holy Ghost, and the Spirit henceforth dwells in him as the SEAL of the living God.

To seal also means "to close up from

sight," to keep privately in reservation. Now God's people are His secret ones. We are told "the foundation of God standeth sure, having this seal; the Lord knoweth them that are His." If God knoweth the number of the stars, and calleth them all by name, how much more intimately knows He His saints who have been bought by the blood of His Son? He knows them, and has sealed them, and in His own time He will bring them forth before the assembled world and prove that they are His. Lastly, the word means to complete. God's people are sealed because they are now, and shall be for all eternity, absolutely complete in Christ. And though indeed they are yet troubled with sin and are yet living in the body of humiliation, God's purposes will ripen fast, and ere long they shall realize their completeness when they reign with Him in light. Believers, St. Paul says, were sealed unto THE DAY OF REDEMPTION, (Eph. iv. 30,) that is, according to the second meaning given above, they are kept to the day of glorious completion, and this fact is strikingly brought out in the Revelation, where both in the 7th and 9th chapters we read that no tempest of wrath is allowed to sweep over the earth until God's people, being publicly sealed, are thereby exempted from its power.

The Holy Spirit is also the Divine *Unction* with which every believer is anointed. " Now He which stablisheth us with you in Christ, and hath *anointed* us, is God." This anointing is the indwelling of the Holy Ghost in the hearts of believers, and is called the " unction from the Holy One." St. John tells us that this unction " abides" in us, and that by it we " know all things," for that " it teacheth us all things, and is truth, and is no lie." (1 John ii. 20, 27.) All believers have this anointing, " for if any man have not the Spirit of Christ he is none of His." All believers therefore have the *fruits* of the Spirit, which are love, joy, peace, long suffering, gentleness, goodness, faith, meekness, temperance ; but the measure of these fruits will vary according to their faithfulness, some bearing only thirty, while others produce sixty and even an hundred fold. Now this anointing is not for spiritual power and edification only, it is to office also. As under the Levitical economy men were anointed to be *priests* and kings, so now believers are anointed to be "a holy priesthood, to offer up spiritual sacrifices, acceptable to God by Jesus Christ." They are also anointed to be *kings*, hence Peter calls the whole Church "a royal priesthood," and St. John says in his ascription of glory: " Unto Him who loved us, and washed us from our sins in His own blood, and hath made us Kings and Priests unto God and His Father; to Him be glory and dominion forever and ever. Amen."

The Holy Spirit is also the Pledge. By the word in the original is meant the "earnest" of what we are hereafter to receive. St. Paul says: "Who hath also sealed us, and given the earnest of the Spirit in our hearts." (2 Cor. i, 22.) In Ephesians, after saying that we were *sealed* by the Holy Spirit of promise, he adds: "which is the earnest of our inheritance until the redemption of the purchased possession." By which he means that the Holy Spirit is in us as a foretaste of what we are hereafter to receive in the fulness of glory. So also the same idea is found in Romans: "Not only they, but ourselves also, which have the *first fruits* of the Spirit, even we ourselves groan within ourselves, waiting for the adoption, to wit, the redemption of our body." (Chap. viii. 23.) I might indeed speak of the Holy Spirit in many of His other offices, but I only mention these in order to shew the reader how mighty is the work of the Holy Spirit in the growth of the believer.

Finally, I only wish to add that progress is the great law in God's kingdom of grace. Nicodemus when he came to Christ was surely but a bruised reed and smoking flax. There was indeed no strength in him, but the day came when this same man openly avowed his love for Christ, and confessed Him, when Israel had crucified, and His own disciples had deserted Him. Peter in his weakness trembled at the voice of a maid, but the day came when he was willing to stretch out his hands and die a martyr for the faith. Paul too grew in grace, and this is apparent especially in the deepening of his humility, for, as Vaughan has pointed out, we find the

Apostle in A.D. 58 writing to the Corinthians that he "was not meet to be called an *Apostle*." In 62 he tells the Ephesians, he is "less than the least of all *saints*," and finally, a year before his death, we find him describing himself to Timothy as the "chief of *sinners*." This was real progress, and such as we ought all to make. If, however, we do desire to grow in grace, like those I have just mentioned, let us all remember that the one great principle of spiritual progression is, ever to keep the eye fixed on the Lord Jesus Christ as the Author and Finisher of our faith.

www.ingramcontent.com/pod-product-compliance
Lightning Source LLC
Chambersburg PA
CBHW021943160426
43195CB00011B/1206